# PIONEERS
## of Physics

by Marie Nestor

PEARSON
Scott
Foresman

DK

# What You Already Know

Everything on Earth is made up of some kind of matter. There are more than one hundred different kinds of matter. Each type of matter is called an element. An element cannot be broken down into pieces by ordinary physical or chemical processes. Every element has a set of physical and chemical properties that can help scientists identify it. Some physical properties are color, smell, texture, mass, volume, and hardness. Chemical properties describe how materials change into other materials.

An atom is the smallest particle of an element that still has all the chemical and physical properties of that element. Atoms are made up of three parts: protons, neutrons, and electrons. Protons and neutrons are located in the nucleus, or center, of the atom. Protons have a positive electrical charge and neutrons have no charge. Electrons move around the nucleus. They have a negative charge.

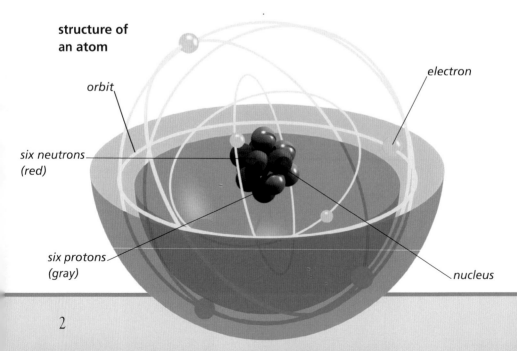

**structure of an atom**

orbit

electron

six neutrons (red)

six protons (gray)

nucleus

When elements are put together they form compounds. The smallest part of a compound is a molecule. The atoms of a compound are held together by the electrons that they share. The physical and chemical properties of a compound are different than the properties of the elements they are made from. Each compound has a name and formula. The compound named water has the formula $H_2O$.

**simple molecule (water)**

When you dissolve one material into another you get a solution. The dissolved material is called the solute. The material it dissolves into is called the solvent. In a saturated solution, the solvent contains as much solute as it can hold. A concentrated solution is almost saturated. A dilute solution is not close to being saturated.

In the following pages you will learn how the pioneers of physics have helped us to learn about matter and its properties.

**complex molecule (sucrose)**

# Matter and Energy

Matter and energy are all around us. Every object you see is made up of matter, from the book in your hands to the stars in the sky. Whenever something moves, or produces heat, light, or sound, there is energy present. The branch of science that deals with matter, energy, and how they work together is called physics.

Over the years, scientists have learned much about how matter and energy make our universe work. Physicists study all forms of energy and matter. They use their observations to come up with rules that describe why matter and energy behave the way they do.

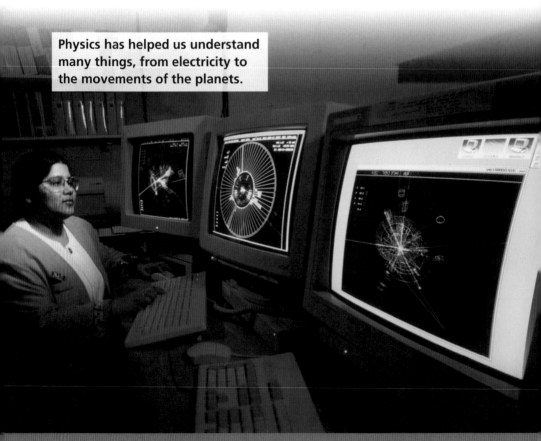

Physics has helped us understand many things, from electricity to the movements of the planets.

**Aristotle** 384–322 B.C.

Aristotle lived more than two thousand years ago. He believed that the mysteries of science could be unlocked by observation. Aristotle encouraged his students to look at the world around them and use reason to decide what their observations meant. The philosophy of observation has become the basic principle behind the study of all sciences.

These rules can then be used to figure out what is happening in new situations. They can also be used to invent new devices and processes. Without an understanding of physics, we could never have invented the light bulb or the automobile.

The study of modern physics began more than four hundred years ago, when an Italian scientist named Galileo Galilei started to wonder about the way objects moved. Back then scientists did not know that Earth rotates around the Sun with the eight other planets. They did not know that gravity is the force that keeps the planets in their orbits. No one understood what electricity was, or how it could be used.

Today we take all of this knowledge for granted. We learned all of these things because of men and women who looked at their world and wondered how it worked. Let's take a look at the lives of some of these famous physicists.

# Galileo Galilei
## 1564–1642

One of the earliest physicists was an Italian man named Galileo Galilei. Galileo studied the sky and wondered about the movement of Earth and the Sun.

Galileo was born on February 15, 1564, in Pisa, Italy. His father wanted him to be a doctor, so in 1581 Galileo was sent to the University of Pisa to study medicine. But he was not interested in becoming a doctor, and soon left the university to study mathematics.

Galileo used his knowledge of mathematics to discover things about the world around him. He observed a chandelier that provided light in Pisa's cathedral. The heavy chandelier swung slowly back and forth on a chain attached to the ceiling. Galileo noticed that each swing took the same amount of time. He used this observation to design the pendulum clock, which uses a pendulum, or swinging weight, to measure time.

**Galileo designed a pendulum clock, although he never built one.**

If you drop a feather and an apple from the same height at the same time, which hits the ground first? The apple, of course! Galileo discovered that the only thing that keeps light objects from falling at the same speed as heavy objects is the air. The feather does not push through the air as easily as the apple. If the air were removed, they would fall at exactly the same speed!

**All objects fall at the same speed if there is no air to slow them down.**

Galileo is probably most famous for his discoveries about Earth and the Sun. He was the first scientist to observe the night sky with a telescope. Using his observations and his knowledge of mathematics, Galileo concluded that Earth and all the planets revolve around the Sun. This was not a new idea at the time, but what Galileo saw through his telescope proved it. Unfortunately for Galileo, this idea was very unpopular. He was forced to stop telling people about it, and was eventually confined to his house. At the time of his death in 1642, most scientists did not accept his theory.

# Robert Boyle
## 1627–1691

Robert Boyle was born in 1627 and raised in Ireland, although his parents were English. Boyle was the seventh of fifteen children.

His parents were very wealthy and could afford to send their children to excellent schools. After the death of his mother, Boyle and his brothers were sent to Eton College in England. Boyle was very popular at school, but left Eton in 1638 to study under private tutors. With one of these tutors, young Boyle went to Florence, Italy, where he visited the home of Galileo. Boyle was inspired by Galileo's work and began to study physics.

Boyle is best known for discovering that squeezing a gas into a smaller space will raise its pressure. Today this is know as Boyle's Law.

As the bicycle pump forces air into the small space of the tire, the pressure of the air increases.

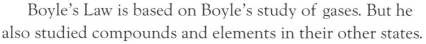

## John Dalton 1766–1844

John Dalton began working more than one hundred years after Robert Boyle, but he used many of Boyle's ideas in his own research. Dalton proposed that all matter is made up of atoms. He said that every element is made up of a different type of atom.

**Dalton's wooden model atoms**

Boyle's Law is based on Boyle's study of gases. But he also studied compounds and elements in their other states.

In 1661 he published a book titled *The Skeptical Chemist*. At the time, people believed that everything in the universe was made up of four "elements": water, air, earth, and fire. Boyle rejected this idea and proposed a definition for elements that we use today.

Boyle declared that elements are materials that cannot be broken down into anything simpler through chemical processes. He stated that elements are the simplest form of matter and can only be found with scientific experiment.

Today Boyle is recognized as one of the fathers of modern chemistry. He believed that the study of chemistry is dependent on the principles of mathematics. Boyle thought that the whole universe could be explained by logical mathematical laws.

# Isaac Newton
## 1642–1727

Sir Isaac Newton was born in
Woolsthorpe, England, in 1642.
Newton attended Trinity College,
Cambridge, where he was a good, but
not outstanding, student. But around
1665, during a break from school,
Newton started to study mathematics and physics on his
own. The discoveries he made established him as one of the
most important scientists of all time.

Newton studied motion and light. He quickly discovered
that light can be diffracted, or spread, when it passes through
a prism. It diffracts into a spectrum of color, which looks
like a rainbow. Newton then tried passing single colors of
this spectrum through the prism. They could not be
diffracted. So he concluded that white light is made up
of many pure colors.

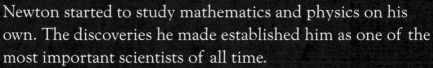

Isaac Newton discovered
that white light is actually
made up of all the colors
of the spectrum.

Newton is most famous for his study of gravity. He wondered what kept the Moon spinning around Earth, and came to the conclusion that they were attracted to each other because of the force of gravity.

Newton's study of gravity led him to develop three laws of motion. The first law states that an object in motion will stay in motion unless acted upon by an outside force. This means that a rolling ball will keep rolling until something stops it, such as contact with the air or ground.

The second law of motion explains that force is equal to the mass of the object times its speed. Heavy, fast-moving objects have more force than light, slow-moving objects.

Newton's third law states that if you put force on an object, it will put an equal force back onto you. This law explains how rockets fly. When the engines push downward at one end, an equal force pushes the rocket in the opposite direction, up into the air.

Atlantis

**A rocket's flight can be explained by Newton's third law of motion.**

# Michael Faraday
## 1791–1867

Michael Faraday was born to a poor English family in 1791. At the age of fourteen, Faraday went to work for a bookbinder. He had an amazing thirst for knowledge so he read every book in the shop.

As an adult, Faraday made very important discoveries about how electricity can be generated, changed, and used to produce movement.

**Faraday giving a lecture**

**Faraday invented the electric generator, which allows us to produce electricity for electric lights.**

Faraday knew that flowing electricity could produce magnetism. He wondered if magnetism had an influence on the flow of electricity. He did an experiment to test his idea and found out that he was correct. In the process, he also invented the transformer, a device that changes the strength of electric currents. Faraday used his new knowledge to

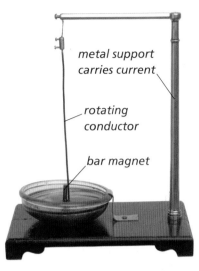

metal support carries current

rotating conductor

bar magnet

**Faraday's electric motor**

build the first generator, which used moving magnets to produce electricity. He called this process electromagnetic induction. Later, he invented the electric motor, which is basically a generator working in reverse. Instead of using movement to produce a current, it uses current to produce movement. As he experimented further with electromagnetism, he found that very strong magnetic fields had an affect on light.

# James Clerk Maxwell
## 1831–1879

James Clerk Maxwell was a physicist and mathematician who built on the ideas developed by Michael Faraday. He was a brilliant scientist from a young age. He wrote a scientific paper for the Royal Society of Edinburgh, Scotland, when he was just fourteen!

Maxwell's study of mathematics led him to come up with several equations to better understand light as an electromagnetic wave. An electromagnetic wave is a wave of energy. Faraday had discovered that light could be affected by electromagnetism. Maxwell concluded that light itself must be a type of electromagnetic wave.

### Heinrich Hertz 1857–1894

Heinrich Hertz added to the work of Maxwell. He was the first to discover radio waves and then determined that they are another type of electromagnetic wave, similar to the ones Maxwell studied.

Maxwell's mathematical equations helped him to determine how light travels. Light is an electromagnetic wave because it is made up of a series of electric and magnetic fields. An electric field generates a magnetic field right next to it. Then that magnetic field generates a new electric field. This happens over and over, like a wave traveling across the ocean.

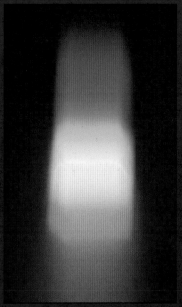

**visible part of the electromagnetic spectrum**

Maxwell studied other areas of science as well. He came up with theories about Saturn's rings. These ideas were confirmed about one hundred years later by a modern space probe. Maxwell did research on color vision and color blindness. His work on color led to the world's first color photograph.

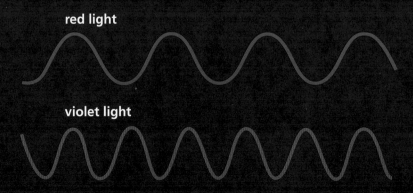

red light

violet light

**Differently shaped waves produce different colors of light.**

# Marie Curie 1867–1934

Marie Curie was born Maria Sklodowska in Warsaw, Poland, in 1867. She studied mathematics, physics, and chemistry in Paris between 1891 and 1897. It was during this time that she married Pierre Curie. The two worked together, along with Antoine Henri Becquerel. In 1903 the three were awarded a Nobel Prize for their work with the radioactivity of uranium.

Certain elements, such as uranium, give off a special type of energy called radioactivity. These elements have very large molecules. The molecules' size makes them unstable, and some of their particles are always flying off in streams. It is these streams of particles that make up radioactive rays. Radioactive elements are very rare.

**Marie Curie eventually became very sick from contact with radiation.**

With her husband and Becquerel, Curie studied radioactive materials and attempted to learn how their rays could be harnessed and used in medical treatments.

The Curies and Becquerel were pioneers in a field that came to be called nuclear physics. Their findings paved the way for the development of nuclear energy.

Curie also discovered the radioactivity of the element thorium, and discovered two new elements. She was awarded another Nobel Prize on her own. But her contact

**Radium molecules are unstable. They are constantly giving off radioactive particles.**

with radioactivity eventually resulted in leukemia, a type of cancer. Marie Curie died in July of 1934 at the age of 67.

Marie Curie's name will forever be remembered in the field of nuclear physics. Today we measure radioactivity in units called curies.

## Antoine Henri Becquerel
### 1852–1908

Antoine Henri Becquerel discovered radioactivity by accident. At first he believed that radioactive materials stored and released sunlight. But when he found that the materials still released energy when kept in a dark drawer, he realized the energy came from the materials themselves.

# Ernest Rutherford
## 1871–1937

Ernest Rutherford was another scientist who studied radioactivity. He was born in 1871 in Nelson, New Zealand.

At the age of sixteen Rutherford entered Nelson Collegiate School. In 1889 he went on to the University of New Zealand, where he studied mathematics and physical science. He graduated in 1893. Later he studied in England and went on to work at McGill University in Canada. Eventually, Rutherford returned to England to teach. In 1908 he was awarded the Nobel Prize in chemistry for his work with radioactive particles.

Rutherford died in Cambridge on October 19, 1937.

**Rutherford (right) worked with Hans Geiger. Geiger introduced an instrument for measuring radiation that we now call a Geiger counter.**

Ernest Rutherford is remembered for his great contributions to the field of nuclear physics, including the discovery of how the parts of atoms are arranged.

Rutherford's research concluded that an atom is arranged like the solar system. He determined that the center of an atom, the nucleus, is positively charged and acts similarly

**Rutherford suggested that negatively charged electrons orbit around a positively charged nucleus inside an atom.**

to the Sun at the center of the solar system, holding the rest of the planets in orbit. The positively charged nucleus holds negatively charged electrons in orbit around it. This basic model of the atom is still used today.

## J. J. Thomson 1856–1940

J. J. Thomson was the first scientist to truly begin to understand what the structure of an atom really looked like. He found out that the electrons are much smaller and lighter than whole atoms. Rutherford used this knowledge to come up with his model of the atom.

# Lise Meitner
## 1878–1968

Lise Meitner was born in Vienna, Austria, on November 7, 1878.

Meitner began her career working at the Kaiser-Wilhelm Institute in Berlin, Germany, where she studied nuclear physics. In 1917 Meitner became head of the institute's physics department. During this time Meitner worked with another scientist named Otto Hahn. The two discovered the element protactinium. Protactinium is a very rare radioactive element that was later used to make the fuel for nuclear power plants.

In 1938 Meitner left Germany, which was under the control of the Nazi Party. She moved to Stockholm, Sweden, where she took a job at the Nobel Physical Institute.

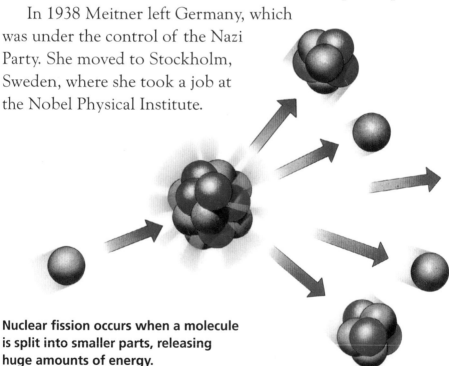

**Nuclear fission occurs when a molecule is split into smaller parts, releasing huge amounts of energy.**

During her career Meitner also discovered that the nuclei of uranium could be split. This process is called nuclear fission and releases a huge amount of energy. Today, this energy is used in nuclear power plants to generate electricity.

During World War II nuclear energy was being studied in hopes of building the first nuclear bomb. Meitner was asked to take part in this research, but she refused.

In 1947 Meitner went to work at a new laboratory started by the Swedish Atomic Energy Commission. Here she worked on developing a nuclear reactor for use in power plants.

Lise Meitner later moved to England, where she died on October 27, 1968.

**Meitner's notes on nuclear fission**

**In a nuclear power plant, the energy of nuclear fission is used to produce electricity.**

# Albert Einstein
## 1879–1955

Albert Einstein was born in Germany in 1879. He received his Ph.D. in Bern, Switzerland, and later moved to Princeton, New Jersey. There he worked at the Institute for Advanced Study, winning the Nobel Prize for physics in 1921.

Einstein's greatest achievement was his general theory of relativity. This theory changed the way physicists understand gravity. Einstein proposed that all objects are surrounded by curved fields of gravity. He suggested that rays of light passing a huge object, such as the Sun, would be bent by the powerful gravitational field. A British scientific expedition observed this during a solar eclipse in 1919. Einstein's theory was proven correct.

**Einstein's work led to a better understanding of how matter and energy are related.**

Einstein is most famous for his equation, $E=MC^2$. This equation explains the nature of energy and matter. Einstein proved that under extreme conditions, matter could be converted directly into energy, which was important to the study of nuclear physics.

Today Albert Einstein is recognized as one of the greatest minds in physics. But he is just one in a long line of scientists who have all taken the advice of Aristotle and looked to the world around them. The study of science continues to advance because great minds keep asking questions about the world around us and searching for the answers. Physicists look to the work of those who have come before them and continue to build on that knowledge, in hopes of creating a better world for future generations.

## Stephen Hawking 1942–

Stephen Hawking uses the theories of Albert Einstein in his study of black holes. Hawking is currently the world's leading expert on black holes and their role in the universe. He continues to build on Einstein's work to discover the rules by which the universe works.

# Glossary

**diffracted**    the spreading of light by a prism

**electromagnetic wave**    a wave of electric energy

**electromagnetism**    magnetism produced by an electric current

**nucleus**    the center of an atom

**prism**    a piece of glass or other clear material that bends light

**radioactivity**    energy produced by large, unstable molecules releasing streams of particles

**spectrum**    a series of bands of colors in order of their wavelengths